D0150543

Put Beginning Readers on the Right Track with
ALL ABOARD READING™

The All Aboard Reading series is especially designed for beginning readers. Written by noted authors and illustrated in full color, these are books that children really want to read—books to excite their imagination, expand their interests, make them laugh, and support their feelings. With fiction and nonfiction stories that are high interest and curriculum-related, All Aboard Reading books offer something for every young reader. And with four different reading levels, the All Aboard Reading series lets you choose which books are most appropriate for your children and their growing abilities.

Picture Readers

Picture Readers have super-simple texts, with many nouns appearing as rebus pictures. At the end of each book are 24 flash cards—on one side is a rebus picture; on the other side is the written-out word.

Station Stop 1

Station Stop 1 books are best for children who have just begun to read. Simple words and big type make these early reading experiences more comfortable. Picture clues help children to figure out the words on the page. Lots of repetition throughout the text helps children to predict the next word or phrase—an essential step in developing word recognition.

Station Stop 2

Station Stop 2 books are written specifically for children who are reading with help. Short sentences make it easier for early readers to understand what they are reading. Simple plots and simple dialogue help children with reading comprehension.

Station Stop 3

Station Stop 3 books are perfect for children who are reading alone. With longer text and harder words, these books appeal to children who have mastered basic reading skills. More complex stories captivate children who are ready for more challenging books.

In addition to All Aboard Reading books, look for All Aboard Math Readers™ (fiction stories that teach math concepts children are learning in school); All Aboard Science Readers™ (nonfiction books that explore the most fascinating science topics in age-appropriate language); All Aboard Poetry Readers™ (funny, rhyming poems for readers of all levels); and All Aboard Mystery Readers™ (puzzling tales where children piece together evidence with the characters).

All Aboard for happy reading!

To my book group, my mom and Chuck, and the Gallini family for contributing the concept, experimenting, and taste testing for the Owl Barf Ball recipe.—G.L.C.

To all the defamed animals—P.M.

GROSSET & DUNLAP
Published by the Penguin Group
Penguin Group (USA) Inc., 375 Hudson Street, New York, New York 10014, U.S.A.
Penguin Group (Canada), 90 Eglinton Avenue East, Suite 700, Toronto, Ontario,
Canada M4P 2Y3 (a division of Pearson Penguin Canada Inc.)
Penguin Books Ltd, 80 Strand, London WC2R 0RL, England
Penguin Ireland, 25 St Stephen's Green, Dublin 2, Ireland
(a division of Penguin Books Ltd)
Penguin Group (Australia), 250 Camberwell Road, Camberwell, Victoria 3124, Australia
(a division of Pearson Australia Group Pty Ltd)
Penguin Books India Pvt Ltd, 11 Community Centre, Panchsheel Park,
New Delhi - 110 017, India
Penguin Group (NZ), Cnr Airborne and Rosedale Roads, Albany, Auckland 1310, New Zealand
(a division of Pearson New Zealand Ltd)
Penguin Books (South Africa) (Pty) Ltd, 24 Sturdee Avenue, Rosebank,
Johannesburg 2196, South Africa

Penguin Books Ltd, Registered Offices:
80 Strand, London WC2R 0RL, England

The scanning, uploading, and distribution of this book via the Internet or via any other means without the permission of the publisher is illegal and punishable by law. Please purchase only authorized electronic editions, and do not participate in or encourage electronic piracy of copyrighted materials. Your support of the author's rights is appreciated.

Text copyright © 2006 by Ginjer L. Clarke. Illustrations copyright © 2006 by Pete Mueller. All rights reserved. Published by Grosset & Dunlap, a division of Penguin Young Readers Group, 345 Hudson Street, New York, New York 10014. ALL ABOARD SCIENCE READER and GROSSET & DUNLAP are trademarks of Penguin Group (USA) Inc. Printed in the U.S.A.

Library of Congress Cataloging-in-Publication Data
Clarke, Ginjer L.
Gross out! : animals that do disgusting things / by Ginjer L. Clarke ; illustrated by Pete Mueller.
p. cm. — (All aboard science reader. Station stop 2)
ISBN 0-448-44390-2 (pbk.)
1. Animal behavior—Miscellanea—Juvenile literature. I. Mueller, Pete, ill. II. Title. III. Series.
QL751.5.C55 2006
590—dc22
2006004896   10 9 8 7 6 5 4 3 2 1

CONCORDIA UNIVERSITY LIBRARY
2811 NE HOLMAN ST.
PORTLAND, OR 97211-6099

Gross Out!

Animals That Do Disgusting Things

By Ginjer L. Clarke
Illustrated by Pete Mueller

Grosset & Dunlap

CONCORDIA LUTHERAN SCHOOL
4663 Lancaster Drive NE
Salem, Oregon 97305
503/393-7188

Can you believe it?

This fish catches its food with slime.

This mammal eats its own poop.

It's true!

Some of the creatures in this book
can squirt poison at their predators.
Some of them feast on blood.
Some eat the vomit of other animals.
All of them do disgusting things.
Are you ready to be grossed out?

Chapter 1
Underwater Creatures

A giant blood-sucking creature

lurks in the Amazon River.

Is it a sea monster?

No! It is a **giant leech**.

The giant leech can grow

up to 18 inches long.

That's about as long

as an adult human's arm.

Most leeches cling to their prey

and drink their blood.

Different types of leeches

suck the blood of birds, fish,

mammals, and even humans.

After a leech bites an animal,

the cut keeps bleeding for hours.

But a leech bite is not deadly.

One type of leech is even used by doctors

to help patients heal from operations.

Sea slugs come in many
different shapes and colors.
One type of sea slug has its insides
on the outside of its body.
This sea slug has long, thin tubes
on its back called "cerata."
(Say it like this: sir-AH-tah.)
The cerata are almost clear,
so if you look closely,
you can see through them
to the sea slug's guts.

Some of these guts are part of the
sea slug's digestive system.
Usually the digestive system
is on the inside of an animal's body.
(Just like your stomach and intestines
are inside of you.)
But not on this creature.
Ewww!
The sea slug can use its cerata
to sting predators.

Red-bellied piranhas are very scary fish.

When they smell blood or see a group of fish,

they attack quickly in large numbers.

Their teeth are as sharp as knives.

Piranhas can even bite through bone.

Piranhas will eat anything,

including other fish, rodents,

birds, and sometimes people!

Snap!

These piranhas caught a catfish.

They swarm around the fish.

Blood fills the water as the piranhas

rip the fish to pieces.

They chomp on the meal

and finish it in only 30 seconds.

Sometimes they gulp big chunks

without even chewing.

The **hagfish** is also called a "slime eel."

The hagfish is almost blind.

It mostly eats dead fish.

When a predator comes close,

the hagfish oozes slime.

The slime covers the enemy fish.

The fish dies because it cannot breathe.

Sometimes a hagfish makes so
much slime that it
covers its own body, too.
The hagfish ties itself into a knot
to wipe off the slime.

Chapter 2
Creepy Crawlers

Have you ever seen a **tick** on a dog?

Or maybe you found a tick on your skin

after a walk in the woods.

Ticks drink blood from

mammals, birds, and reptiles.

Before a tick starts eating, it is very small.

It crawls onto an animal or person

and bites with its mouthparts.

After a tick sucks blood,

its belly gets much bigger.

Some types of ticks spread disease
through bacteria in their mouthparts.
When a person gets bitten,
the bacteria infects the person
with a disease.
But the disease can be treated
if the person goes to a doctor soon.

Dung beetles have a nasty diet.

They mostly eat the dung

of other animals.

Dung is another word for "poop."

Dung beetles eat poop!

Dung beetles use their mouthparts
to cut up chunks of poop.
Then they roll the poop into small balls
with their longer back legs.
This beetle carries a ball of poop
like a wheelbarrow
while walking backward.
Dung beetles save the poop balls
and eat them when they get hungry.

You probably know that many spiders
catch prey in sticky webs.

Maybe you have felt a spider's web.

Another bug, the **velvet worm**,

does something even stickier.

It squirts a gluey liquid at its prey.

Pow!

This velvet worm shoots liquid

from two openings on its head.

The gluey liquid dries in seconds.

The insect is trapped.

The velvet worm bites a hole

in the insect's body.

Then the worm injects its saliva.

The insect's insides become soupy,

and the worm slurps them out.

Yummy!

Many animals eat other types of animals.

But some animals eat their own kind.

These animals are called cannibals.

The **praying mantis** is a cannibal.

After these praying mantises mate,

the female mantis turns around.

She is much larger than the male.

She raises her front legs

and grabs the male.

Chomp!

She bites off his head.

How rude!

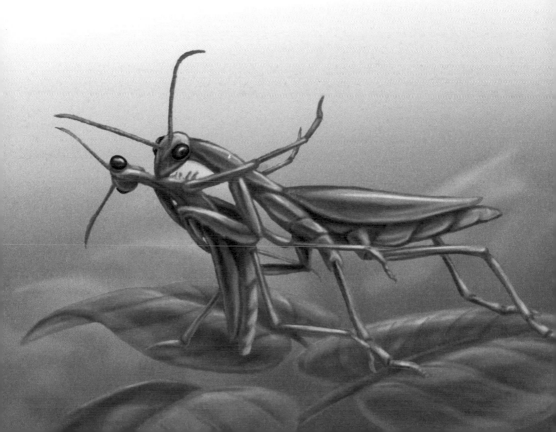

Chapter 3

Reptiles and Amphibians

The **legless lizard**

is also called a "glass snake,"

because it breaks into pieces

when it is attacked.

Just like glass breaks

when it is dropped.

This legless lizard wants

to escape from a bird.

The bird tries to grab the lizard.

The lizard's tail pops off,

and the lizard is free.

But the tail piece keeps moving!

This creepy defense scares

the bird away.

Another lizard protects itself

by being super gross.

When a **horned lizard** is in danger,

it squirts blood out of its eyes.

This does not hurt the horned lizard,
but it really scares its enemy.
This gives the lizard a chance
to run away to safety.

Some animals carry their
babies on their backs.
But one toad actually gives birth
to babies that have been stuck
inside her back!
The **Surinam toad** lives on riverbeds.
After a male and female toad mate,
the male presses the eggs
onto the female's back.
The female toad's back becomes squishy,
and the eggs sink into her skin.

The eggs grow into tiny toads.
A few months later, the toads start to
swim out of their mother's back.
They break their mother's skin
with their tiny front legs.
This does not hurt the mother,
but it sure looks painful!

Many poisonous animals bite their prey.

But the **cane toad** does something different.

It can squirt poison at its enemies

from three feet away!

The poison sprays out of holes

on the sides of the toad's neck.

The poison makes the predator

shake, drool, and puke before it dies.

Even humans can get hurt and sick

if they touch a cane toad.

The cane toad is one of the

largest toads in the world.

It is almost as big as a rabbit.

It will eat any creature

it can swallow.

This cane toad munches a snake.

That's a mouthful!

Chapter 4
Mammals

Do you know which mammal

is nearly hairless, wrinkled, and

almost blind?

A **naked mole rat**.

This animal is related to a guinea pig.

It is also called a "sand puppy."

It sure is funny looking!

And it's gross, too.

Naked mole rats live in groups
in underground burrows.
They use their long teeth
to dig up roots to eat.
But when they are really hungry,
mole rats eat their own poop!
They also roll around in
puddles of their own pee.
Mole rats can tell each other apart
by the smells of their pee and poop.
What little stinkers!

Vampire bats are creepy looking.

They have big ears, squished noses,

and small, sharp teeth.

Most types of bats eat fruit or bugs,

but vampire bats eat only blood.

They drink blood from animals

like birds, pigs, cows, and horses.

Many people are afraid of vampire bats,

but they rarely bite humans.

This vampire bat uses its
spiked fangs to make a cut in
a sleeping cow's leg.
Then the bat licks the cow's blood.
Slurp!

Have you ever heard someone say,
"He's playing 'possum"?
People say that because opossums
are good at pretending to be dead.
This **Virginia opossum** sees a
great horned owl that wants to eat it.
The opossum falls over and stays still.
It hangs its tongue out of its mouth,
so it looks like it is dead.
Then it poops green slime
that smells like rotting flesh.
Phew!

The owl flies away to get

far from this disgusting smell.

The opossum is just fine.

But its trick sure fooled the owl!

There are several types of armadillos.

Most of them are hairless.

But the **hairy armadillo** has

long, thick hairs all over its body.

The hairy armadillo digs under

animals that are dead and rotting

to eat the bugs that live beneath them.

The hairy armadillo will also

eat the dead animal's flesh.

But it has small teeth and

cannot chew very well.

So the armadillo munches on the meat

until it is mushy enough to swallow.

Chapter 5
Birds

Is that a seagull?

No, it is a **fulmar**.

Fulmar means "foul gull."

This bird pukes up disgusting yellow oil
and hurls it at its attackers.

The fulmar can fling its puke up to five feet.

The puke sticks to the enemy bird's feathers
and can cause the enemy bird to drown.

Baby fulmar chicks can vomit

up to one foot away

as soon as they are born.

The chicks even vomit at their parents

until they learn to tell the difference

between their parents and other birds.

Lots of animals take food
from other animals.

But the **magnificent frigate bird**
does something really gross.

The frigate bird does not
dive into the ocean to find fish.

It takes food that other birds
have already eaten.

It steals the puke of other birds!

This frigate bird chases a
blue-footed booby in the air.
The frigate bird pulls on the
booby's tail feathers.
The booby falls off balance and
throws up the meal it has just eaten.
Then the frigate bird catches the
booby's puke and eats it before it falls
into the water.
Yuck!

The **harpy eagle** is big and strong.

It can catch and eat large animals

like sloths and monkeys.

Most birds can only eat prey

smaller than themselves.

But the harpy eagle eats animals

almost as big as it is.

Harpy eagles are expert hunters.

They have wingspans up to seven feet wide.

They sit quietly and then dive

through the trees to snatch their prey.

Whoosh!

This harpy eagle swoops down
into the rain forest.

It grabs a howler monkey and carries it off.

Its talons are the size of grizzly bear claws
and can crush the bones of its prey.

Its hooked beak is as sharp as a razor
and can rip off huge chunks of flesh.

This bird is an eating machine!

The **eagle owl** is one of the largest owls.

Its wingspan can be over five feet long.

It is a fast, smart hunter.

The eagle owl catches and eats
many kinds of animals.

Its diet includes snakes, insects,
small mammals, and even other large birds!

This eagle owl holds a vole in its feet.

It pulls the vole apart with its sharp bill.

A vole is a small mammal like a mouse.

The owl eats quickly and swallows

every part of the vole.

After the owl is finished eating,

it throws up a hard pellet.

This barf ball is made of fur, bones,

and anything else the owl cannot digest.

The skeletons of small animals

can even be put back together from

the pieces found in owl barf balls!

Owl Barf Balls

Would you like to fool your friends and tell them they're eating owl puke? It's easy and fun to make this recipe for yummy, pretend owl barf balls. Don't worry—they taste much better than they look!

Always remember to get an adult to help you when you are cooking in the kitchen.

Ingredients:

¼ cup butter (half a stick)

1 cup granulated sugar

¼ cup milk

1 teaspoon cocoa

¼ cup chunky peanut butter

1½ cups oats (not instant oatmeal)

½ cup pretzel sticks (broken into small pieces to look like bones) (optional)

¼ cup coconut flakes (for fur) (optional)

Supplies:

Large wooden or plastic spoon

Medium saucepan

Teaspoon

Wax paper

Cookie sheet

Directions:

1. Mix the butter, sugar, milk, and cocoa in the medium saucepan with the large spoon.

2. On the stove, heat the pan on medium high and stir the mixture with the spoon until it is smooth.

3. Bring the mixture to a boil for 1 minute.

4. Turn off the burner and remove the pan from the heat.

5. Add the peanut butter, oats, pretzel pieces, and coconut to the mixture, and stir until combined. Allow mixture to cool for 5 minutes in pan (until it is cool enough to touch).

6. Scoop out the mixture and drop by the teaspoonful onto the cookie sheet lined with wax paper. (Use a little butter or margarine on the teaspoon so the mixture doesn't stick.)

7. Place the cookie sheet in the refrigerator for 10 minutes.

8. Remove the blobs from the wax paper and form into balls.

Store in a container in the refrigerator for up to two weeks or in the freezer for up to two months for fun snacking anytime. Makes 2 to 3 dozen Owl Barf Balls.

The next time you have to eat
something you don't like for dinner,
just be glad you don't have to
steal barf like a frigate bird,
eat poop like a dung beetle,
drink blood like a vampire bat,
or act like any of the animals in this book.
Now that would be *really* gross!